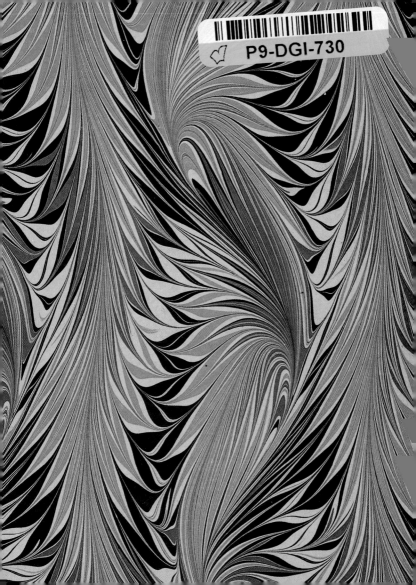

WATER

THE LIBRARY *of* GARDEN DETAIL

WATER

PATRICK TAYLOR

Simon and Schuster

New York   London   Toronto   Sydney   Tokyo   Singapore

Simon & Schuster

Simon & Schuster Building
Rockefeller Center
1230 Avenue of the Americas
New York, NY 10020

Text copyright © 1993 by Patrick Taylor
Photographic credits appear on page 63.

Designed by Paul Burgess
Printed in Singapore by Tien Wah

Library of Congress Cataloging-in-Publication Data

Taylor, Patrick.
 Water/Patrick Taylor.
    p. cm—(The Library of garden detail)
 ISBN 0-671-79690-9
 1. Water in landscape architecture.   2. Gardens—Design.   3. Water gardens.   I.
Title.   II. Series.
SB475.8.T39   1993
714—dc20
                                                          92-26408
                                                            CIP

10 9 8 7 6 5 4 3 2 1

CONTENTS

$\mathcal{I}$ N T R O D U C T I O N

N O GARDEN CAN EXIST WITHOUT WATER, WHETHER IT springs from the ground or falls from the sky. From the Book of Genesis onwards ('And a river went out of Eden to water the garden; and from thence it was parted, and became into four heads'), all gardens have used water, either as an absolute necessity for growing plants, or as an ornament to delight the eye and ear, or as a symbol of life itself. Water lay at the very heart of the paradise gardens of the Near East, which were introduced to the south of Spain with the coming of Islam. The Moorish Patio de los Leones in the fourteenth-century Alhambra has a central fountain from which water flows along four runnels under the shady arcades that surround it. Muslims treated water like a precious material, not merely the essence of life, but something beautiful in itself, to be used with relish in fountains, gushing springs, intricate water runnels, and formal sheets of water reflecting liquid light into the deep shady recesses of their palaces. In the orange garden beside the Mezquita (mosque) in Cordoba – probably the oldest continually gardened site in the world – the straight rows of trees are irrigated by an elegant pattern of stone-lined runnels opening out into circles about the trunk of each tree. Spaniards use water as an integral part of their gardens – public and private – to this day.

8

In late medieval Christian gardens, such as those shown in such loving detail in Flemish fifteenth-century minia-tures, a fountain, symbolising the spring of life, and thus the Virgin Mary, is often placed at the centre. The name Mary, of course, comes from *mare*, the Latin for sea. The association of water with ideal femininity is also found in classical mythology (Venus born from the waves) and in Chinese symbolism where water and mountains were taken to represent the Yin and Yang, complementary opposites, the feminine and masculine. The Chinese for landscape is *shan shui*, 'mountains and water' – the vital ingredients of classical Chinese gardens, where intricate shapes of weather- or water-worn rocks rising mountain-like from

9

1. *In Spain the sound of splashing water in a shady patio is an essential part of the character of Moorish courtyard gardens.*

symbolic water in the form of a sea of swirling raked sand, formed the essential garden idea. Incidentally, although real water often appeared in classical Chinese gardens it was almost always used in an entirely naturalistic way; formal fountains and water ornaments were found only in the Imperial gardens which were regarded by purists as rather vulgar and ostentatious. Water in the form of rain or mist was also regarded as an important garden ingredient. Mary Keswick, in her wonderful book *The Chinese Garden*, writes: 'The Kao-ts'ung Emperor of the Ch'ing dynasty, for instance, made a special trip to a celebrated island garden known as the *Lou* of the Misty Rain. When he arrived the sun shone brilliantly, the waters sparkled and the outlines of the isle shimmered in the heat. It was a perfect day; and the Emperor was deeply disappointed.'

In Japan, too, the subtle symbolism of water determined garden aesthetics. There was an exact typology of cascades: ten kinds for use according to the vigour of the water-flow, from *tsutai*, water rippling over stones for a gentle flow, to *kasane-ochi*, for a copious stream, in which water tumbles precipitously over a series of high steps. The sound of water was important in the Japanese garden; in

10

order to produce a lively splashing a stream might be narrowed at a certain point to concentrate the flow of water, and rocks placed to interrupt it. Another character-

2. *Japan is successfully evoked in a Philadelphia garden. Against a background of gnarled bark of an old pine, a bamboo spout feeds a stone font carved into a lotus shape and moss and hostas relish the moist shade.*

11

istic Japanese device was a bamboo pipe dripping water into a calm pool and gently disturbing its surface.

As far as the western tradition of gardening is concerned, it was the Renaissance in Italy that had the greatest influence on the way in which water was used in gardens. Water was disciplined in channels, it erupted from fountains, it cascaded down elaborate water-steps linking

3. *A successful and subtle modern arrangement in which changes of level and varied materials are cleverly interwoven.*

terrace after terrace and falling to great calm pools. Water to Renaissance man was not merely ornament or symbol, it was also an essential part of the study of physics. The science of hydraulics was harnessed to produce all sorts of wonderful water-powered machines and garden ornaments.

12

Agostino Ramelli's *Le diverse e artificiose machine* ('Diverse ingenious machines'), published in 1588, is ostensibly a textbook of hydraulics, but it shows how water power may be used to animate garden ornaments – twittering birds, moving figures and dramatic sound effects, not to mention the ingenious water tricks to wet the unwary. In the garden at Pratolino near Florence, made in the 1570s and probably the most famous garden of its day, there was a vast Mount Parnassus, the dwelling of the muses, with a water-powered organ playing music. John Evelyn visited Pratolino in 1645 and wrote: 'the gardens are delicious and full of fountains. . . . All these waters come from a rock in the garden, on which is the statue of a gyant representing the Apennines.' Giambologna's immense statue still survives. Evelyn also saw a tunnel formed by jets of water so high that 'a man on horseback may ride under it and not receive one drop of wet'. At the Villa d'Este, Tivoli, the architect Pirro Ligorio laid out the greatest water garden ever made, where visitors may still see a dazzling aquatic firework display. Here, as in other Italian gardens of the Renaissance, the exuberance of immense fountains is contrasted with the calm of shady pools.

The great Italian gardens of the sixteenth century were influential throughout Europe; they provided a repertoire of ideas on which all formal gardens in Europe have drawn since. Grand tourists visited, adapted the ideas and recreated them in their own countries, sometimes to bizarre effect. A garden of terraces, fountains and cool pools – perfect for Tuscany – may have a rather different atmosphere in, say, North Wales. But in the latter part of the eighteenth century at Monticello in the hills of west Virginia Thomas Jefferson found a terrain and a climate that suited well the villa idea which inspired him in his garden making.

In some countries the lie of the land did not provide the natural fall of water that was so essential to Italian gardens and so easily found in the Tuscan hills. At Het Loo, William III's palace in the eastern Netherlands, water for the 45ft high King's Fountain was piped from higher ground six

4. *The giant Brazilian rhubarb,* **Gunnera manicata,** *unfolds its spectacular pleated foliage. This great plant absolutely demands a watery woodland setting.*

miles away to provide the necessary pressure. At Versailles there was never enough water to keep all the fountains

5. *Bold water-lily pads enliven the surface of this ornamental raised canal fed by water jets from a bold stone dolphin.*

going at once. The great Machine de Marly, built on the banks of the Seine in 1680, had 14 waterwheels powering a huge pump, to provide water for Marly and Versailles; but even this was not enough. It required a team of garden boys, signalling to each other with whistles and turning stop-cocks at appropriate moments, to give the impression to Louis XIV's well marshalled guests that fountains played without cease throughout the garden.

Italian Renaissance gardens borrowed from classical mythology to provide suitable subjects to ornament watery places. Nymphs peopled grottoes, Neptune rose above frolicking dolphins and Venus erupted from the waves. In countries less learned in the detail of classical mythology, later books had to explain the rules that governed the placing of garden statues. Batty Langley's *New Principles of Gardening* (1728) ridiculed classically illiterate gardeners for putting '*Neptune* on a terrace-walk, Mount, &c. or *Pan*, the god of sheep, in a large Basin'. In different periods the same subjects take on different identities. The river gods of the sort found at the Villa Lante and the Villa Farnese (Caprarola) – sprawling figures holding vessels from which water endlessly springs – were based on classical Roman figures. When they arrived at Versailles they were transmuted into the Great Rivers of France (the Loire, Rhône, etc); in the Netherlands, at Het Loo, similar figures were identified with the Rhine and the Ijssel – which run on either side of the Het Loo estate; by the time the idea had reached England the river god had become the symbol of the piddling River Stour, shivering in a grotto at Stourhead.

In the English landscape garden, water, in the form of a river and a lake, was a vital ingredient, and the grotto, a feature of Renaissance gardens in Italy, gained a new lease of life as the dwelling place of watery deities – Neptune, river gods and nymphs. Whereas the Italian Renaissance grotto was usually either connected to, or near the villa or great house, the English eighteenth-century landscape garden grotto was moved to the very shores of a lake – at, for example, Claremont, Painshill or Stourhead. At the same period, however, Thomas Jefferson, though well versed in fashionable European garden ideas, chose as the only water feature at Monticello a characteristic blend of the ornamental and the functional: a pair of circular fish ponds, around which curved the sinuous shape of his 'roundabout walk' edged with flower beds.

6. A well judged fringe of clipped myrtle and paving of sea pebbles, gives emphasis to a small formal pool in a garden on the Côte d'Azur.

In the nineteenth century a great garden innovation in Britain was the carefully planted but naturalistic stream or pool. Osgood Mackenzie at Inverewe on the north-west

20

7. *The stately calm of a vast lily pool in this Edwin Lutyens and Gertrude Jekyll garden is enriched by superb brick and stonework.*

coast of Scotland had decorative pools in his woodland garden, densely planted with tender exotics. From 1885 onwards, William Robinson at Gravetye Manor took a special interest in the planting around the banks of two lakes, where he introduced alders, dogwoods, poplars, willows, bulrushes (and other reeds and grasses), ferns, flags and loosestrife.

Later in the nineteenth century a revival of interest in gardens with a strong architectural character stimulated a renaissance of more formal water features. The gardens of Edwin Lutyens and Gertrude Jekyll were dazzlingly inventive in their use of water. At Hestercombe, in Somerset, England, for example, water flows from grotesque masks to feed long slender runnels planted with irises, and ultimately into square lily pools; and in an enclosed circular garden Lutyens made a perfectly circular pool which mirrors the ornate surrounding masonry richly planted with wintersweet and rambling roses.

Water has been treated with great imagination in

8. *Lively and varied planting in a New York State garden makes an exciting contrast to placid waters edged with the majestic swaying fronds of ornamental grasses.*

twentieth-century American gardens. At the brilliant Naumkeag in Massachusetts, Fletcher Steele laid out a seductive 'afternoon garden', an out-of-doors room whose centrepiece was an oval pool surrounded by lotus-shaped basins with jets of water. Steele designed exceptional swimming pools, deftly integrating them into the decorative schemes of his gardens, with the occasional female figure lurking in a shady nymphaeum. At Dumbarton Oaks in Georgetown, Beatrix Farrand laid out a garden in the 1920s which made much of water, including a vast pebble mosaic shimmering in shallow water, and, at the centre of a rondel of clipped hornbeam, an elaborate fountain and pool.

In modern gardens there is often a dispiriting timidness and, worse still, a twee-ness in the use of water. There are too many little kidney-shaped pools flaunting their crisp fibreglass contours and garnished with water-lilies struggling for existence in stagnant water showing about as much sparkle as a bucket of sump-oil. Mass-produced watery gew-gaws – lions' masks spouting water, shivering concrete nymphs, mean jets of water – spread an atmosphere of gloom.

Yet water may still be used with great effect in even the smallest garden. In a town garden, a little pool will bear welcome reflections of the sky and bring light and sparkle to a shaded corner. Francis Bacon, writing in his essay 'Of gardens', disapproved of pools: 'Pools mar all and make the garden unwholesome and full of flies and frogs'; and certainly, still water needs much maintenance. Any garden débris must be scrupulously removed; vital oxygen must be added by means of a circulating pump or by growing water plants; and the presence of fish, glinting decoratively in the shallow water, wonderfully animates a pool. A simple fountain – it is unwise to attempt something in the style of André Le Nôtre unless your garden is on the scale of Versailles – may make an excellent eyecatcher and give the soothing sound of tinkling water, cooling a hot summer's evening. On a grander scale, a narrow canal or runnel, edged with stone or concrete slabs and ornamented with pots, can make an effective axis in a modest-sized formal garden. If you are lucky enough to have natural running water in your garden there are few more satisfying ways of gardening than planting moisture-loving plants – from primulas to the splendid giant rhubarb, *Gunnera manicata*,

9. *Water spouts from a lead winged figure, bringing a note of formality to the leafy edges of this pool.*

which only looks remotely at home in a wild and watery setting.

Waterfalls are difficult to arrange unless your garden is on a slope and you happen to have a stream or a sufficiently grand garden to permit a formal cascade. But a gentle flow of water (circulated by a small and, one hopes, silent electric pump) falling over rocks into a simple pool fringed with ferns and moss is a satisfying ornament that is not hard to achieve and gives much of the essence of the waterfall idea.

26

A natural water feature – a pool or a stream – can determine the character of a garden. But the introduction of an artificial water feature must be done with discretion. Whether you are flooding a valley to make a lake, or lining a hole to make a pond, it should be appropriate, both in scale and in type, and should fit harmoniously into the overall design of the garden. Nothing enlivens a garden so much as water. Splashing or dripping, glistening ripples over stone, or reflections on a smooth surface, all can give a liveliness and tranquillity that no other garden feature can provide.

ℛUNNING
𝒲ATER

27

10. *A well planned stream edged with mossy rocks has a lively spring planting of candelabra primulas (*Primula florindae*) and columbines (*Aquilegia vulgaris*).*

28

11. *A brilliant vista in which formal design is blurred by generous planting. Slabs of stone make simple bridges, enticingly criss-crossing the water, and a distant figure provides an eyecatcher.*

12. *A moist ditch in spring, with only a trickle of water, provides the perfect conditions for ferns, Welsh poppies and clumps of* **Euphorbia polychroma** *in this Surrey water garden designed by Gertrude Jekyll.*

13. *A dashing scarlet Japanese bridge veiled by a weeping willow lends a brilliant oriental note to an English garden set among water meadows on the river Avon – such artifice makes nature seem even more natural.*

14. *A shallow, winding stream is richly planted with white, cream and yellow bearded irises (*Iris germanica *cultivars) in the Ladew Topiary Gardens in Maryland.*

32

15. *Brilliant yellow marsh marigolds (*Caltha palustris*), bog arum (*Lysichiton americanum*) and irises make a harmonious spring planting, all freshness and sparkle, on the banks of this little stream.*

16. *A fast-moving hillside brook threads its way between mossy stones edged with hostas, willows, irises and pale drifts of daffodils – nature improved by the deft hand of the gardener.*

17. *Drama is provided by bold rocks strewn in the bed of this stream in a Pennsylvania garden. The scattered leaves of maples make a brilliant autumn picture.*

𝒥NFORMAL

𝒫OOLS

18. *In the Japanese garden at Courances in France the autumn foliage of Japanese maples and the leaf-scattered turf running down to the water's edge give emphatic oriental character.*

36

19. *Early morning mist and the low sun slanting through drifts of spring bulbs gives powerful atmosphere to the water lying naturally in the graceful contours of a scoop of land.*

20. *An arching Japanese bridge garlanded with white and violet wisteria spans Monet's lily pool at Giverny – the subject of many of his paintings and now brought vividly to life in a brilliant restoration.*

38

21. *Sections of tree trunks in Japanese style make a lively edging and underline the oriental character of the plantings of Asiatic rhododendrons and azaleas.*

39

22. *Pink* Geranium endressii *and rich purple irises give colour to the mossy green fringes of this little woodland pool.*

40

23. *The bold foliage of hostas, like frozen waves, and strong stony shapes make a powerful frame for this pool in Pennsylvania.*

24. *The tropical setting of this leafy Bermudan pool is given startling character by exotic plantings of the great sacred lotus,* Nelumbo nucifera, *with its spreading glaucous foliage and curious flowers.*

42

25. Grass and mossy rocks make a naturalistic border to this informal
pool surrounded by lavish woodland planting.

26. *Lavish groups of moisture-loving plants crowd in, all but obliterating the sparkling surface of the water – a miniature jungle in a New York State garden.*

44

27. *A glint of water, only just visible among profuse plantings of candelabra primula and feathery astilbes, sketches the essential idea of a woodland pool transposed to the garden.*

𝔉ORMAL

𝔓OOLS

28. *A brilliant example of the ornamental use of a swimming pool – note its sombre lining, infinitely more satisfactory than the commonly seen blue-green. Clipped box shapes echo the curves of the Lutyens seat which stands out crisply against the yew hedge.*

46

29. *A circular lily pool fits snugly into this crowded and romantic
arrangement. A central water jet, silver thistles and a profusion of white
roses sparkle against sombre yew hedges.*

30. *An oriental atmosphere is powerfully achieved with simple and bold ingredients. Water bubbles over a flat disc, giving lively movement at the centre of a symmetrical arrangement of bricks, seats and trellis.*

31. *The reflections in a mirror-like expanse of water add a special visual dimension to a garden. The sky is brought closer and new views are opened on the surrounding plantings.*

32. *Here, a bold sweep of water is emphasized by a fringe of* Iris kaempferi *and contrasts with the billowing upright form of a weeping silver pear (*Pyrus salicifolia *'Pendula') and clipped yew hedges.*

33. *In a small garden in Philadelphia a spouting mask feeds a simple brick-edged pool whose surface is splashed with water lilies.*

34. There is an exotic Moorish atmosphere about this curvaceous pool whose boldly scalloped stone edging imitates the shape of the lily pads.

52

35. *At Barnsley House vivid blue* Iris sibirica *and sharp yellow* Iris
kaempferi, *both moisture-loving plants, crowd in about this pool,
overlooked by a pillared temple.*

36. *The effect of brilliant autumn colours is doubled by reflections in the water. Rough stone walling and abundant planting blurs the formality.*

ℱOUNTAINS

& ℱONTS

*37. A beautifully contrived wall font in this Belgian garden is given an
architectural setting softened by bold-leafed ivy and pots of arum lilies
(Zantedeschia aethiopica).*

38. *The movement of tumbling water splashing from the dolphin's mouth gives life to this little stone figure.*

56

39. *Dramatic vistas of splashing water jets and circular pools set in a fine architectural framework give a powerful Italian flavour to this English terraced garden.*

40. *A raised fountain and miniature pool in this sunny herb garden make a striking ornament and give vertical emphasis to the horizontal plantings of purple sage, silver wormwoods and irises.*

58

41. *Here, in this Philadelphia garden, a*
mischievous-looking horned goblin spouts water
into a little brick-edged pool, bringing the sparkle
of moving water to a confined space.

42. *A lead font in a shady, moist place is fringed with plants of striking foliage –* Hydrangea petiolaris, *silver dead nettle (*Lamium*) and hostas.*

43. *Brilliant blue tiles of Moorish character, the* azulejos *of Andalusia,
fringe a pool in California. In a shady grotto behind, ferns and ivy are
glimpsed, clinging to the moist stones.*

44. *Lively stonework surrounds this niche in an English garden,
beautifully designed by the architect F. Inigo Thomas. Water jets from
an urn and falls over moss-covered stone to the pool below.*

S O U R C E S

Some US Addresses

**Florida Aquatic
Nurserie, Inc.**
700 South Flamingo Road
Fort Lauderdale, FL 33325
Telephone: (305) 472-5120

**Lilypons Water Gardens,
Inc.**
6800 Lilypons Road
P.O. Box 10
Buckeystown, MD 21717-
001
Telephone: (301) 874-5133

**Matterhorn Nursery,
Inc.**
227 Summit Park Road
Spring Valley, NY 10977
Telephone: (914) 354-5986

**Shady Lakes Water Lily
Gardens**
11033 Hwy 85 NW
Alameda, NM 87114
Telephone: (505) 898-2568

Tranquil Water Lily
4761 Olive Street
San Diego, CA 92105
Telephone: (619) 263-9965

Water Garden Gems
Rt. 2, Box 65
Marion, TX 78124
Telephone: (512) 659-5841

Contact your local chamber
of commerce for other
sources in your area.

Some UK Addresses

**Gardener's World and
English Water Gardens**
London Road
Washington
West Sussex
RH20 3BL
Telephone: 0903 892006

Stapeley Water Gardens
Stapeley
Nantwich
Cheshire
Telephone: 0270 623868

62

P I C T U R E   C R E D I T S

The publisher thanks the following photographers and organizations for their kind permission to reproduce photographs in this book.
Owners and designers of gardens are credited where known.
Photographers appear in bold type.

Title page: **Patrick Taylor**; Cuzco, Spain
page 6 **Andrew Lawson**; Private garden, Oxford
Picture No 1 **Patrick Taylor**; Cuzco, Spain
Picture No 2 **Derek Fell**; Swiss Pines Garden, PA, USA
Picture No 3 **Eric Crichton**; Private garden, Surrey
Picture No 4 **Jerry Harpur**; Geoffrey Dean (designer) Bunbury, Shropshire
Picture No 5 **Andrew Lawson**; York Gate, Leeds
Picture No 6 **Jerry Harpur**; Claus Scheinert and Thomas Parr (designers) 'La Casella', near Grasse, Alpes-Maritimes
Picture No 7 **Andrew Lawson**; Folly Farm, Berkshire
Picture No 8 **Jerry Harpur**; Wave Hill, NY, USA
Picture No 9 **Patrick Taylor**; Wayford Manor, Somerset
Picture No 10 **Jerry Harpur**; 'Quietways', Kentmere, near Kendal, Cumbria
Picture No 11 **Jerry Harpur**; Sir Geoffrey Jellicoe (designer) Michael and Lady Ann Tree, Shute House, Dorset
Picture No 12 **Andrew Lawson**; Vann, Surrey
Picture No 13 **Eric Crichton**; Lady Anne Rasch, Heale House, Wiltshire
Picture No 14 **Derek Fell**; Ladew Gardens, MD, USA
Picture No 15 **Andrew Lawson**; Docton Mill, Devon
Picture No 16 **Andrew Lawson**; Docton Mill, Devon
Picture No 17 **Derek Fell**; Swiss Pines Garden, PA, USA
Picture No 18 **Hugh Palmer**; Courances, France
Picture No 19 **Andrew Lawson**; Private garden, Buckinghamshire
Picture No 20 **Andrew Lawson**; Monet's Garden, Giverny
Picture No 21 **Eric Crichton**; Private garden, Surrey
Picture No 22 **Andrew Lawson**; The Gables House, Somerset
Picture No 23 **Derek Fell**; Jamison Garden, PA, USA

63

64